Contents

Documents Resource Book

1 Introduction to the Documents-Based Questions — 2

2 Answering the Documents-Based Questions — 3

3 Case Studies: Additional Documents-Based Questions

    Case Study 1: The First Programme for Economic Expansion, 1958–63 — 11

    Case Study 2: The Impact of RTÉ, 1962–72 — 17

    Case Study 3: The Impact of the EEC on Fisheries — 22

4 Government, Economy and Society in the Republic of Ireland, 1949–89

    Key Concepts and Other Significant Terms — 27

5 Key Personalities — 32

MODERN IRELAND 3RD EDITION

Introduction to the Documents-Based Questions

The compulsory documents-based topic for students sitting the Leaving Certificate Examination in 2018 and 2019 is *'Government, Economy and Society in the Republic of Ireland, 1949–1989'*. Students are required to answer four compulsory documents-based questions in Section 1 of the examination paper. The questions are based on one of three case studies:

- The First Programme for Economic Expansion, 1958–63
- The Impact of RTÉ, 1962–72
- The Impact of the EEC on Fisheries

In the documents-based question, students are tested in four key areas:

1. **Comprehension:** In this type of question students are required to locate information in the given documents and to provide answers that are short, factual and relevant.
2. **Comparison:** Here the student is required to compare two or more documents on the same event and to identify the similarities and differences between them.
3. **Criticism:** In answering this question, students are expected to comment critically on the usefulness and reliability of documents and, for example, to identify the presence of bias or propaganda.
4. **Contextualisation:** This type of question tests the ability of students to relate the events described in the document to the wider historical context.

In the allocation of marks, there is a higher weighting for the comprehension section at Ordinary Level and a higher weighting for the contextualisation section at Higher Level.

Document Type

At both Ordinary and Higher Level two documents from one case study are usually chosen. These documents may be written or visual and consist of primary and/or secondary sources.

Primary sources may include:

- visual sources such as photographs or cartoons
- newspaper accounts
- letters and diaries
- interviews and speeches
- autobiographies and memoirs
- government records or reports.

Secondary sources may include:

- biographies
- books written by historians.

 Answering the Documents-Based Question

The documents-based question is in Section 1 of the examination paper and is normally answered first. It is important to remember that students have about 40 minutes to answer this section of the paper. At Higher Level students should spend 20 minutes answering Questions 1–3 and 20 minutes answering Question 4, which deals with contextualisation. At Ordinary Level 15 minutes should be allocated to Question 1 and 25 minutes to Questions 2–4.

In answering the documents-based question, students should note the following:

- Read Question 1, which deals with comprehension. This enables you to approach the documents with specific questions in mind.
- Read the document carefully.
- Underline key relevant words and sentences.
- Answers to Question 1 on *comprehension* should be direct, short and relevant.
- In answering Question 2 on *comparison*, it is important to refer to both documents and to note both differences and similarities between them. Refer to examples from the documents when answering this question.
- In answering Question 3 on *criticism*, be mindful of the difference between primary and secondary sources, the viewpoint of the author of the document, and the presence or absence of bias or propaganda. Refer to evidence from the documents to support your assertions.
- Question 4 on *contextualisation* tests your knowledge and understanding of the wider historical background of the case study. In answering this question, you should ensure that your answer is relevant to the question asked and shows an appreciation of key issues, personalities and events.

Read through the following selection of documents from your textbook, together with the model answers provided. Then practise your answering skills by reading and responding to the documents in the next section of the resource book.

Example 1 – Case Study 1: The First Programme for Economic Expansion, 1958–63

Study Documents A and B below and read the questions and model answers that follow.

Document A: The Need to be Competitive

> *If we do not expand our production on a competitive basis, we shall have failed to provide the economic basis for the political independence and material progress of the community. Indeed, if we expect to fail, it would be better to make an immediate move towards re-incorporation in the United Kingdom rather than to wait until our economic decadence became even more apparent.*
>
> *For these reasons the importance of the next five to ten years for the economic and political future of Ireland cannot be over-stressed. Policy must be re-shaped without regard to past views or commitments.*

Source: *Economic Development*, Dublin: Department of Finance 1958

Document B: T. K. Whitaker's Tribute to Seán Lemass

> *I must say it was a very pleasant surprise when the Fianna Fáil Government, committed so much to self-sufficiency and protection, abandoned it all so readily. There is no doubt that Lemass was the great moving dynamic spirit in all of this. There was grudging acquiescence, or recognition granted, that without Lemass's drive and also probably without de Valera's benevolent blessing, change would not have come about nearly as quickly. Lemass was a pragmatic nationalist, and I put the emphasis on the two words. He was a nationalist in the sense of wanting to see Ireland have a respectable place in the world, but I don't think he was opposed to Dev's traditionalist outlook. He simply had some impatience with it in so far as it might be a hindrance to change, the change he wanted. He didn't have a programme of cultural change. His aim, as indeed my own, was focused on improving the economic and social scene.*

Source: T. K. Whitaker, cited in J.F. McCarthy (ed.), *Planning Ireland's Future: The Legacy of T.K. Whitaker*, Dublin, Glendale 1990, 52–3

Comprehension

1. (a) According to the author of Document A, what was required to 'provide the economic basis for the political independence and material progress of the community'?

    Answer:
    Ireland would need to expand production on a competitive basis.

(b) What, according to the author of Document A, should be ignored when re-shaping policy?

Answer:
Past views or commitments should be ignored.

(c) According to the author of Document B, what had the Fianna Fáil government abandoned all so readily?

Answer:
A commitment to self-sufficiency and protection.

(d) What aim did the author of Document B share with Seán Lemass?

Answer:
Both men were focused on improving the economic and social scene in Ireland.

Comparison

2. (a) In what way are both Documents A and B similar in expressing the need for economic change in Ireland?

Answer:
In Document A it is stated that government policy must be changed and not held back by ideas from the past. Likewise, in Document B it is stressed that Lemass was committed to achieving economic change and progress.

(b) Does Document A or Document B give you greater insight into the achievements of Seán Lemass?

Answer:
I think that Document B provides more information. Although Document A is a primary source, it is identifying the problem of the Irish economy. Document B, on the other hand, gives an understanding of the role of Seán Lemass as seen by the central figure working alongside him, T.K. Whitaker.

Criticism

3. (a) How successful is the author of Document A in conveying a sense of urgency around the need for economic progress?

Answer:
The author conveys this well by remarking that Ireland would have failed as an independent state if the economy did not improve.

(b) Is Document B a biased source? Explain your answer.

Answer:
It is clear from his praise that T.K. Whitaker was a great admirer of Seán Lemass. However, he justifies his statements, and despite the fact that he worked closely with Lemass, I would not regard it as a biased source.

Contextualisation

4. In what ways was the Irish economy transformed between 1958 and 1963?

Answer:

Between 1958 and 1963 the Irish economy experienced huge growth and expansion. This was in marked contrast to the stagnation and economic depression of the 1950s. By 1956 around 40,000 people were emigrating every year. At a time when Britain and countries in Western Europe were experiencing huge economic growth, the economy in Ireland was hardly growing at all. The policy of economic protection enforced since 1932 had failed to provide enough jobs for the population. To many it seemed as if the independent Irish state was an economic failure.

Two men in particular are associated with the radical transformation which took place from 1958 onwards: the Taoiseach, Seán Lemass; and the leading civil servant, Dr T.K. Whitaker. Appointed secretary of the Department of Finance in 1956, Whitaker drew up a report on the state of the Irish economy. This was the origin of the *First Programme for Economic Expansion* published by the Fianna Fáil government in 1958. When Lemass became Taoiseach the following year he implemented the programme with enthusiasm.

The First Programme set out specific targets for agriculture and industry over the following five years. Economic protection was abandoned in favour of free trade, and generous tax concessions encouraged foreign companies to set up factories in Ireland. The programme aimed for 2% growth a year in the economy, but it actually resulted in a 4% growth rate. Huge expansion in Irish exports wiped out the balance of payments deficit. Increased levels of employment resulted in a fall in emigration and an increase in the population.

The growth in the economy and rising revenue from taxes enabled the government to invest more in areas such as health and education. At the same time Irish people became more hopeful for the future. While the economic progress laid the foundation for a changing society, not everyone benefited to the same degree.

Example 2 – Case Study 2: The Impact of RTÉ, 1962–72

Study Documents A and B below and read the questions and model answers that follow.

Document A: A *Late Late* Controversy: Audience Joins Heated Debate

> *There were heated interjections from the studio audience during the* Late Late Show *on Telefís Éireann last night, and at one stage a spectator said to Gay Byrne: 'I think it is up to you Mr Byrne to stop characters coming up here to slag the clergy.' Gay Byrne instantly replied: 'Wait a minute. I do not bring people in here to slag the clergy. We have a programme and we are proud of it as a programme on which you are allowed to say what you want.'*

Trinity College student and playwright, Brian Trevaskis, who appeared as a member of the panel, referred to Galway's new cathedral as 'a ghastly monstrosity'. In a city which did not have such things as a theatre or art galleries the people were having to pay for this monstrosity.

He added: 'I don't blame the people of Galway – I would rather blame the Bishop of Galway.' Referring to the celebration of the fiftieth anniversary of the 1916 Rising, he added that the Constitution had guaranteed equal rights and equal opportunities for all our citizens. One man who tried to achieve this was Dr Noël Browne, but the Archbishop of Dublin had put back the image of Ireland from fifty to one hundred years

A member of the studio audience rose and said: 'The people from where I come from – Ballygarvan, County Cork, would not listen to you speaking so degradingly about our Churches and Bishops'. Another member of the audience said he thought Mr Trevaskis spoke a bit harshly, but he was glad to see he was not afraid to express his opinions.

Another member of the audience . . . said he thought Mr Trevaskis was right in his criticism, and he agreed that Ireland had developed very little since the Proclamation. 'I support Brian as a progressive member of the youth of Ireland,' he said. **99**

Source: *Sunday Press*, 27 March 1966

Document B: The Search for Balance

66 *They tell me, the historians know about such things, that when the history of Ireland for the next fifty years comes to be written, television in general and the* Late Late Show *in particular will be mentioned as having been a tremendous force for change in the community . . . 'Broadening the horizons' and 'letting in fresh air' are two of the phrases thrown around like snuff at a wake.*

One of the things which this programme has done to me is to deprive me of the luxury of ever having only one point of view about anything; give me a man who has an opinion about something and by tomorrow morning I'll produce ten men who will disagree with him. And they will all fiercely resent the other being allowed to speak.

When one is producing television programmes, one is reminded forcefully and regularly that there are two sides to every story, and the depressing thing is that when you try honestly to present those two sides, you very quickly discover that there are another two you hadn't dreamed of.

MODERN IRELAND 3RD EDITION

> *In fifteen years of radio and television I have never been able to find out what balance is. I only know that 'lack of balance' is when anyone gets up and says anything a politician disagrees with. When a Fianna Fáil man comes along and congratulates me on a job well done and tells me that I have achieved a 'balance', I know precisely what he means. He means thank God that shower from Fine Gael and Labour never got a chance to get a word in. The only trouble is that as soon as he's gone both of the other two are screaming at me about 'lack of balance' and about programmes which are a disgrace and an affront to Irish viewers. It is quite astonishing the number of people in this country who are firmly convinced that they have a God-given mandate to speak on behalf of the nation.* 🙴

Source: Gay Byrne, *To Whom It Concerns: Ten Years of the* Late Late Show, Dublin, Gill & Macmillan 1972, 158–60

Comprehension

1. (a) In Document A, what did Brian Trevaskis call the new cathedral in Galway?

Answer:
He called it a ghastly monstrosity.

(b) What accusation did he make against the Catholic archbishop of Dublin (Dr John Charles McQuaid)?

Answer:
Trevaskis claimed that the Archbishop had damaged the image of Ireland by putting it back from 50 to 100 years.

(c) According to the author of Document B, what will future historians have to say about the *Late Late Show*?

Answer:
They will mention it as a tremendous force for change in the community.

(d) At the end of Document B, what does the author describe as 'quite astonishing'?

Answer:
He finds it astonishing that so many people believed that they had a God-given right to speak on behalf of the nation.

Comparison

2. (a) How do both Documents A and B show the importance of controversy on television?

Answer:
Document A gives a lively example of a dispute between Brian Trevaskis and members of the audience over the actions of Catholic bishops in Ireland. Likewise, in Document B, Gay Byrne mentions the importance of airing opposing points of view on the *Late Late Show.*

(b) Which of the two documents gives a better impression of a clash of opinions on television?

Answer:

In my view Document A is better at this because it is a primary source and we can read what the opposing characters actually said on the night in question.

Criticism

3. (a) How effective is Document A as a primary source?

Answer:

I find Document A very good at conveying what actually happened. It is a newspaper account and it gives the different points of view and the words actually spoken by the people involved in the controversy.

(b) Is Document B an unbiased source?

Answer:

No. I believe that Gay Byrne expresses his own point of view strongly in this document. He is clearly annoyed at the behaviour of people on the show who refused to listen to opposing points of view. He mocks them in the final sentence by saying that such people believe that they have a God-given right to speak on behalf of the nation.

Contextualisation

4. How did RTÉ respond to a changing society during the 1960s?

Answer:

RTÉ was to the forefront in the changing society of the 1960s. When Irish television first broadcast on 31 December 1961, many politicians, including the Taoiseach, Seán Lemass, did not realise how it would influence Irish society in a more liberal direction. Lemass believed that RTÉ should show support for the government of the day and that it should not enjoy complete independence. As broadcasters believed that people were entitled to hear all sides of controversial topics, tension was soon to arise between the station and politicians.

RTÉ responded to the desire of people for more and deeper treatment of current affairs by expanding its news coverage and establishing special programmes such as *Seven Days*. When programmes gave equal weight to supporters and opponents of the government, conflict could arise. For example, the Minister for Agriculture, Charles Haughey, intervened to object to the amount of coverage given to his opponents during a dispute with farmers in 1966. The government set up an enquiry when a *Seven Days* programme on illegal money lending used hidden cameras. However, the most serious example of government action would take place concerning events in Northern Ireland.

When the Troubles broke out in Northern Ireland people in the Republic were interested as violent events unfolded, and RTÉ crews were on the spot to film them.

People were no longer content to read about these developments in newspapers, but instead tuned in to television coverage. When some of the participants were interviewed on RTÉ, the Irish Government became concerned. In 1971 the Minister for Posts and Telegraphs, Gerard Collins, put Section 31 of the Broadcasting Act into operation and ordered the station not to interview people who carried out or supported violence in Northern Ireland. An interview with a leading member of the IRA, Seán Mac Stiofáin, led to the dismissal of the RTÉ Authority by the Minister.

Of all the programmes on RTÉ, the *Late Late Show* with presenter Gay Byrne was the most controversial. It responded to changes in society as more and more people desired open and frank discussion of controversial issues. Unlike previous generations, who had lived in a society marked by censorship and the very strong influence of the Catholic Church, people in the 1960s increasingly wished to make up their own minds on social and moral issues. In a *Late Late Show* programme a panellist, Brian Trevaskis, criticised the Catholic Archbishop of Dublin and the Catholic Bishop of Galway. Many people in the studio audience defended the bishops. Gay Byrne believed that such open discussion was a healthy development in Irish society.

The high number of foreign programmes shown on RTÉ was also a response to a changing society. Irish people were interested in lifestyles in the USA and Britain, and American and British programmes attracted large numbers of viewers. Critics complained about the damage being done to Irish culture by foreign influences.

Historians speak of the developments of a global village when describing the influence of television in modern societies. As a result of RTÉ programmes Irish people were able to see scenes from life in Africa, Asia and the USA brought into their own living rooms.

Documents Resource Book

3 Case Studies: Additional Documents-Based Questions

CASE STUDY 1
The First Programme for Economic Expansion, 1958–63

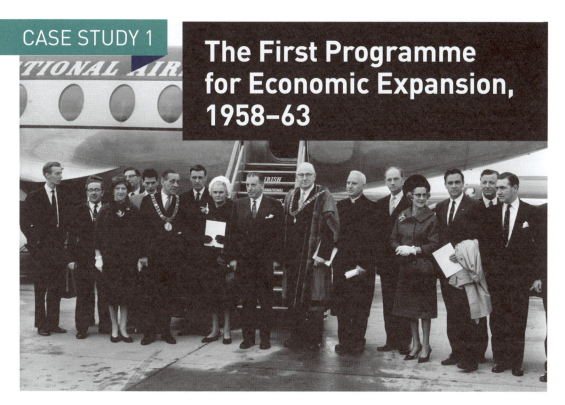

In this case study students are expected to examine and understand documents related to Ireland's economic development between 1958 and 1963. In particular, they should understand the contribution of Seán Lemass and T.K. Whitaker. Students should learn about the First Programme for Economic Expansion in the wider context of political and social change. See the textbook (pages 278–285) for a detailed account of these developments.

Read the following sets of documents related to this case study and answer the questions that follow.

Document A: A Dublin Opinion Cartoon (July 1956)

Document B: A Businessman's View of the Gloom of Poverty in the Late 1950s

> We in Ireland are beginning to throw off the pall of gloom that has been darkening our days, confusing our minds and our policies and distracting our intelligence and our energies. I sense it in many walks of life . . . The doctrine of our poverty and lack of material resources continues to plague our people like a dark and brooding medieval superstition . . . It is not merely among workers or small farmers that this doctrine survives, but among the educated in business and commerce in industry and agriculture . . . The doctrine of poverty destroys hope and where there is no hope there is no courage . . . This myth of our inevitable poverty must at all costs be destroyed.

Source: speech by Joseph Griffin reported in the *Irish Press*, 20 November 1958

Questions

Comprehension

1. (a) In Document A, what was the noticeboard intended to represent?
   (b) What message did it convey about the state of the Irish economy in the 1950s?
   (c) According to the author of Document B, what doctrine plagued the lives of Irish people?
   (d) How did this doctrine affect Irish society?

Comparison

2. (a) What does the view of Ireland's economic problems in Document A have in common with the view expressed in Document B?
   (b) Which document expresses the more pessimistic view?

Criticism

3. (a) How effective was the cartoonist in Document A in conveying the problems facing Ireland in the 1950s?
   (b) State one strength and one weakness of Document B as a source for the historian.

Contextualisation

4. What role was played by T.K. Whitaker in Ireland's economic development?

Document C: The Challenges Facing Lemass on Becoming Taoiseach in 1959

> **"** The historical task of this generation, as I see it, is to consolidate the economic foundations of our political independence. These foundations are not by any means firm enough to be certain of their permanency. The task of consolidating and extending them cannot be postponed. It has got to be done now or in the years immediately ahead of us. This, I believe, is the crucial period in our attempt to build up an Irish state which will be capable of maintaining permanent independence. If we fail, everything else goes with it and all the hopes of the past will have been falsified. But if we succeed, then every other national problem including particularly the problem of partition, will become a great deal easier of solution. **"**

Source: *Dáil Debates*, 3 June 1959

Document D: Economic Progress under Lemass

> *Irish investors became visibly more confident from 1960 on. Net emigration was lower between 1961 and 1966 than during any period since independence. Under the First Economic Programme, economic growth was deliberately projected pessimistically at 2% per annum; actual rates of 4% were achieved. Industry was again the star, and in 1961 a historically unprecedented overall growth rate of 8% was recorded. Even without government action, people were keeping their children in school for longer and were waking up gradually to the value of education in the post-agrarian world that Ireland was belatedly entering . . . In 1961 Fianna Fáil was returned to office as only a minority government by the electorate, despite this upturn in the country's fortunes . . . Many have claimed that the minority government of 1961–5 was the best the country had ever seen. Certainly, this government presided over a period of unprecedented prosperity, a prosperity that generated a consumer society of sorts for the first time in history.*

Source: T. Garvin, *Judging Lemass*, Dublin, Royal Irish Academy 2009

Questions

Comprehension

1. (a) In Document C, what did Seán Lemass see as the main task facing the Irish people?
    (b) What did he see as the benefits of succeeding in this task?
    (c) State two indicators in Document D of Ireland's economic progress under Lemass.
    (d) What view does the author express regarding the minority government under Lemass between 1961 and 1965?

Comparison

2. (a) According to Document D, how effective was Lemass's response to the challenges he identified in Document C?
    (b) How do Documents C and D differ as sources for the historian?

Criticism

3. (a) What did Lemass's speech in Document C reveal about his vision of the future of Ireland?
    (b) What view of Lemass as Taoiseach emerges from Document D?

Contextualisation

4. How effective was Seán Lemass in bringing about economic change in Ireland in the 1960s?

Document E: The Legacy of Seán Lemass: A Historian's Point of View

There was significant achievement in the short period. Yet there were also distinct limitations to the legacy of Lemass, even in his chosen socio-economic field. Industrialisation had advanced gradually. But Lemass did not solve the problem that had baffled him since 1932 – how to create a viable Irish industry. By the mid-sixties, the continuing failure of Irish-owned industry on the export front, despite all the incentives, was becoming grimly clear. Only the success of foreign investment was now energising the export drive. The hope that foreign example would inspire native emulation was proving vain . . . The subsidies seem to have been largely squandered. At least they did not achieve the objective of making Irish industry competitive . . .

Despite these emerging problems, Lemass bequeathed a far more promising legacy than the one he inherited. The forces of resistance remained powerful. But they were coming under challenge for the first time since independence . . . The generation that came to manhood and womanhood in the 1960s was the first in more than a century to have a realistic chance of making a decent living in their own country. Only time would tell what they would make of it.

Source: J.J. Lee, *Ireland 1912–1985: Politics and Society*, Cambridge University Press 1989

Document F: The 1960s as a Golden Era: The Critical Eye of the Historian

Although there may be a tendency to exaggerate the economic success of Ireland in the 1960s (it was not very high by European standards), it was certainly the case that national poverty no longer sufficed as an excuse for social neglect. There was also a new generation coming to the fore – in politics, the media, health services, sport, musical, cultural and legal life, and religion – who seemed to have little patience with or tolerance of conditions their elders had endured, and they refused to indulge in the sanctification of deprivation which had persisted in some quarters of Irish nationalist thinking . . .

It was that sense of optimism which has coloured the view of Ireland in the 1960s as confidently swinging . . . No doubt the reappearance of economic depression and emigration in the 1980s heightened the perception of the 1960s as a golden era, given the virtual absence of emigration that had become a standard feature of Irish life since independence . . . For all the steps taken forward, there was still much stagnation and class snobbery . . . In a small open economy much of the wealth generated served to widen the gulf between rich and poor.

Source: D. Ferriter, *The Transformation of Ireland 1900–2000*, London, Profile Books 2005

Questions

Comprehension

1. (a) According to the author of Document E, what did Seán Lemass fail to solve?
   (b) What is the author's views of the generation that came to manhood and womanhood during the 1960s?
   (c) According to the author of Document F, what was the attitude to poverty of the new generation in the 1960s?
   (d) What impact did the generation of wealth in the 1960s have on the divisions between rich and poor?

Comparison

2. (a) What do Documents E and F convey about the opportunities enjoyed by the generation of Irish people growing up in the 1960s?
   (b) How are Documents E and F similar as sources?

Criticism

3. (a) In your view, does the author of Document E present a balanced assessment of the economic achievements of Seán Lemass? Explain your answer.
   (b) Does the author of Document F present an uncritical view of Ireland in the 1960s as a 'golden era'?

Contextualisation

4. What social and economic changes took place in Ireland during the 1960s?

Documents Resource Book

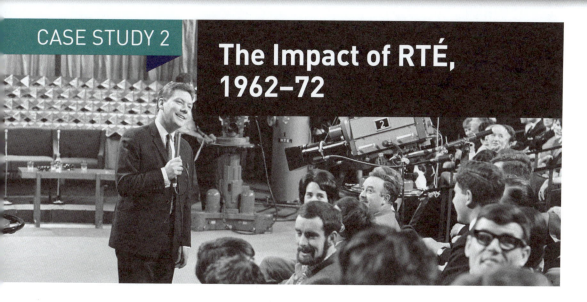

CASE STUDY 2
The Impact of RTÉ, 1962–72

In this case study students are expected to read and understand documents which concern the impact of RTÉ on Irish society in the first decade of the country's native television service. In this regard they need to have an understanding of the impact of RTÉ on the social and cultural development of the country. The textbook (pages 299–310) gives a detailed account of these developments.

Document A: 'American Influence'

"Even the interference seems to have a certain amount of American influence."

Source: *Dublin Opinion*, January 1962

MODERN IRELAND 3RD EDITION

Document B: The Cultural Impact of Television: A Historian's Viewpoint

> *Television exercised a pervasive influence. The state had 438,000 TV licences on 31 December 1970 compared with only 93,000 on 31 March 1962. The fact that the opening of an Irish television station coincided with the spread of a questioning mentality and a receptivity to change among the public increased its potential influence further. Television helped to promote a capacity for self-criticism by asking awkward questions, pulling back the edges of carpets, exposing feet of clay. Over 50 per cent of RTÉ television broadcasting featured imported programmes at the end of the 1960s. In 1971 nearly 90 per cent of children's programmes were imported. When combined with the impact of British television, which could be viewed along the east coast, this probably did more in a decade to anglicise, or to Anglo-Americanise, Irish popular culture than the official anglicisation policies of centuries of British government.*

Source: J.J. Lee, 'Continuity and Change in Ireland, 1945–70' in J.J. Lee (ed.), *Ireland 1945–70*, Dublin, Gill & Macmillan 1979

Questions

Comprehension

1. (a) What view of Irish television does Document A convey?

   (b) How did the cartoonist portray this in the image of the television screen?

   (c) According to the author of Document B, which trends in Irish society coincided with the opening of RTÉ?

   (d) State two pieces of evidence from Document B which show the extent of foreign programmes on Irish television during the 1960s.

Comparison

2. (a) What aspect of the impact of RTÉ on Irish society is expressed in both Document A and Document B?

   (b) Set down two differences between Documents A and B as sources on the impact of RTÉ for the student of history.

Criticism

3. (a) How effective is Document A in conveying a particular point of view?

   (b) What do you consider to be the strengths of Document B?

Contextualisation

4. What role did RTÉ play in exposing Irish society to foreign influences?

Document C: 'Political Interference'

"It's the Minister. He says that, while he objects to the item, and will raise hell if it's inclued, he is in no sense to be taken as bringing any pressure to bear."

Source: *Dublin Opinion*, November 1966

Document D: Politicians and Broadcasters

> Ireland was in transition from de Valera's Ireland to that of Lemass. And the latter's government in introducing the new television service, rather inattentively entrusted to the broadcasters more independence than Lemass himself may have suspected was wise. He often stated that he might revisit this legislation were he dissatisfied with how the broadcasters exercised their responsibilities. What Lemass failed to appreciate was that the public approved of a television service with this degree of independence. Once the genie was out of the bottle, there was no going back. Lemass remained grumpy about what he saw as a television station that did not know its place: what he failed to appreciate was what an ally it would prove in accelerating his own modernising agenda.

Source: J. Bowman, *Window and Mirror: RTÉ Television: 1961–2011*, Cork, Collins Press 2011

Questions

Comprehension

1. (a) Who has made contact by telephone with RTÉ? (Document C)
   (b) What message was conveyed?

(c) Why was Lemass not satisfied with RTÉ, according to Document D?
(d) What, according to the author of Document D, did Lemass fail to appreciate?

Comparison

2. (a) Compare the attitude of politicians to RTÉ displayed in Documents C and D.
   (b) Which document conveys more effectively the existence of political pressure on RTÉ? Explain your answer.

Criticism

3. (a) What do you understand was meant by the minister's words in Document C?
   (b) Is Document D a primary or a secondary source? Explain your answer.

Contextualisation

4. What impact did RTÉ have on Irish society between 1962 and 1972?

Document E: Cartoon – Irish Storyteller

'Bí fear ann fadó agus fadó a bí – will ye listen to me!'

Source: *Dublin Opinion*, March 1960

Document F: The Impact of RTÉ on Public Debate

❝ Television had been a growing influence in Ireland since the early fifties, since the British programmes could be received over a considerable portion of the country, including the main population centre, Dublin. But its real importance for Irish culture came with the opening of a national television service, Telifís Éireann, on New Years Day 1962. Television is a medium which requires controversy. A *newspaper can get away with a single, slanted presentation of views for years on end; but a television discussion will be intolerably dull unless the participants disagree with each other.*

Telefís Éireann has come to realise that this applies to religious discussions as much as to any others, and as time has gone on it has allowed increasing freedom of discussion on religious topics. One was Mr. Michael Viney's programme, 'Too Many Children?' broadcast late in 1966, in which Dublin mothers discussed frankly their attitudes to family planning. The other is Mr. Gay Byrne's Late Late Show, *put on every Saturday night throughout most of the year, which is Telefís Éireann's most popular discussion programme, and which often tackles religious topics. If there is much more public discussion among Irish Catholics than there used to be, it cannot entirely be attributed to the influence of the Vatican Council; the factor of a local television service must be taken into account as well.* ""

Source: J.H. Whyte, *Church and State in Modern Ireland 1923–1970*, Dublin, Gill & Macmillan 1971

Questions

Comprehension

1. (a) What message is conveyed by the cartoonist in Document E?
   (b) Why does the storyteller appear to be upset?
   (c) According to the author of Document F, how did Irish television encourage controversy?
   (d) What effect did television have on the discussion of religious topics during the 1960s?

Comparison

2. (a) What view of the impact of television on Irish society is conveyed in both documents?
   (b) Which document do you consider to present a more objective point of view? Explain your answer.

Criticism

3. (a) How effective is the cartoonist in Document E in highlighting the cultural impact of television?
   (b) How does the author of Document F support his view that television is a medium that requires controversy?

Contextualisation

4. In what ways was Irish television controversial during the first decade of its existence?

MODERN IRELAND 3RD EDITION

CASE STUDY 3

The Impact of the EEC on Fisheries

In this case study students are expected to read and understand documents covering the changes to the Irish fishing industry in the 1970s and 1980s. In particular, they should focus on how membership of the EEC affected the development of Irish fisheries. Students should have a knowledge and appreciation of the social and economic impact on fishing communities and on the respective roles of the EEC, Irish Governments and fishermen's organisations. See the textbook (pages 345–351) for a detailed account of these developments.

Document A: Employment in the Fishing Industry

	1970	1980	% INCREASE
FISHERMEN FULL-TIME	1,960	3,485	78%
FISHERMEN PART-TIME	3,900	5,333	37%
FISHERMEN TOTAL	**5,860**	**8,818**	**50%**
SHORE PROCESSING	920	1,600	79%
OTHER FULL-TIME EMPLOYMENT	360	770	114%
TOTAL EMPLOYMENT	**7,140**	**11,188**	**57%**

Source: John de Courcy Ireland, *Ireland's Sea Fisheries: A History*, Dublin, Glendale 1981

Document B: The Expansion of Irish Fishing in the 1970s

> *Ireland has viewed its fishing industry as underdeveloped but with potential for generating economic growth and employment, particularly in peripheral areas where jobs were scarce, incomes low and emigration high . . . The total national catch rose by 89 per cent in volume between 1970 and 1980, while the average price of catches increased by more than 500 per cent during the same decade . . .*
>
> *The hope that development of fishing would generate more employment has been justified. In 1958 there were 1,700 full-time fishermen, plus 4,500 part-timers; by 1981 there was a total of 8,740 fishermen, of whom 3,364 were in full-time employment. Investment in shore-based activities related to fishing continued to grow, so that by the late 1970s some fifty sea-food distribution and processing establishments employed more than 2,500 people.*
>
> *Given the massive increase of investment in this industry – from £5 million in 1970 to £53.5 million in 1979 – the Irish government was obviously concerned to protect the interests of this sector.*

Source: M. Wise, *The Common Fisheries Policy and the European Community*, London, Methuen 1984

Questions

Comprehension

1. (a) According to Document A, which category of fishermen experienced the greater increase between 1970 and 1980?
   (b) How did total employment in the fishing industry change between 1970 and 1980?
   (c) How, according to Document B, did Ireland view its fishing industry?
   (d) Why did the Irish Government want to protect the interests of the fishing industry?

Comparison

2. (a) How was the hope expressed in paragraph 2 of Document B supported by the figures in Document A?
   (b) State one difference between Document A and Document B as sources on the growth of the Irish fishing industry

Criticism

3. (a) Identify one limitation of Document A as a source for the historian.
   (b) Would you regard Document B as a biased or unbiased source? Explain your answer.

Contextualisation

4. How did the Irish fishing industry grow during the 1970s?

Document C: Irish Fisheries and the Regions

> ❝ Over two-thirds of the people who work in the fishing industry live in the regions of the western seaboard. In this region household incomes are lower than the national average. The general rule is that the more the community depends on fishing, the lower its average income tends to be. In Donegal and the north-western region the average household income was £1,399 in 1973, while at the same time the national average was £2,094. ❞

Source: Irish Federation of Marine Industries, *A Pragmatic Study of the Irish Sea-Fishing Industry*, Dublin 1977

Document D: The Economic Importance of the Irish Fishing Industry

> ❝ Historically, it could be said that Ireland has looked more to the land than to the sea as a means of earning a livelihood for its people. Of all the industries I know it is hard to think of another industry which has a better socio-economic and regional profile than fishing, fish farming and its ancillary sectors. Here in Ireland this industry provides a livelihood for over 15,000 people or approximately 1.5% of the labour force. Most of these jobs are located in the remoter coastal regions of a country which is itself on the western periphery of Europe.
>
> Up to one-fifth of those employed on the western seaboard are dependent on fishing and fish farming for their livelihood . . . The sea is often the only resource that can be exploited economically and hence provides a critical role in maintaining and sustaining populations in coastal areas. ❞

Source: A.O. Gannon, 'The Problems of the Irish Fishing Industry' in Sherkin Island Marine Station (ed.) *The Common Fisheries Policy: Mid-Term Review*, Sherkin 1991

Questions

Comprehension

1. (a) According to Document C, in what part of Ireland did most of those working in the fishing industry live?

   (b) What connection did the author of Document C draw between dependence on fishing and average income?

(c) According to Document D, how many Irish people earned their living from the fishing industry?

(d) How important was the fishing industry as a source of employment for those living on the western seaboard?

Comparison

2. (a) Compare the references to the West of Ireland in Documents C and D.

(b) Which document do you consider to be a more useful source? Explain your answer.

Criticism

3. (a) How effective do you think Document C is at highlighting the problems facing the West of Ireland?

(b) Does Document D provide an unbiased account of the importance of the fishing industry?

Contextualisation

4. What problems faced the Irish fishing industry during the 1970s?

Document E: A Profile of Joey Murrin

> *He (Joey Murrin) has worked with 15 successive government ministers, and most of them were afraid of him. Such is his influence that one former political party leader is known to have had 'sudden mood changes' at the very mention of his name. Now Joey Murrin, fishing industry leader, is retiring – 'but', he warned at the opening of Fisheries Ireland 2000 in his home port of Killybegs, Co Donegal, this week, 'I'm not quite going away'.*
>
> *Mr Murrin first came to prominence in 1971 at a time when fishermen felt they were getting a raw deal during Ireland's accession to the European Union. He was working as a deckhand as he had done on various boats from 1954 to 1974. Elected secretary of the then Killybegs Fishermen's Association in 1958, he became its chairman in 1973. The following year, he was voted chairman of the Irish Fishermen's Organisation and served for five years.*
>
> *In 1979, he left to set up the Killybegs Fishermen's Organisation as a producers' body and was also nominated to his first of several terms as director of Bord Iascaigh Mhara. Most observers knew he was destined for politics and, in 1986, the then Taoiseach, Dr Garret FitzGerald, appointed him as chairman of BIM. Dr FitzGerald also asked him to stand for Fine Gael as a European election candidate in Connacht-Ulster.*

Source: *Irish Times*, 7 July 2000

MODERN IRELAND 3RD EDITION

Document F: The EEC's View on Irish Fisheries

It is fair and reasonable as the European Commission has proposed, to reserve a specially favourable treatment for the Irish fishing industry within Community policies. However, it is equally fair and reasonable to suggest that fishermen from other EEC countries, in whose markets and for whose assistance Ireland rightly claims equal treatment, should continue to fish within strictly controlled limits in waters within Irish jurisdiction. Any other approach by the Commission would have been one-sided and unjust.

Source: Finn Gundelach, Vice-President of the European Commission, in a speech at Letterkenny, Co. Donegal, 17 February 1978

Questions

Comprehension

1. (a) Give one example from Document E which shows that Joey Murrin was an influential figure in the Irish fishing industry.
    (b) State two positions held by Joey Murrin.
    (c) According to the author of Document F, did the European Commission treat the Irish fishing industry fairly?
    (d) What view did the author express concerning the fishing rights of other EEC countries?

Comparison

2. (a) How does Document E differ from Document F as a source for the historian?
    (b) Which document most clearly represents a strong point of view? Explain your answer.

Criticism

3. (a) Do you think that the author of Document E provided a sympathetic account of the achievements of Joey Murrin?
    (b) Did the author of Document F present a balanced view on the treatment of the Irish fishing industry within the EEC? Explain your answer.

Contextualisation

4. What impact did EEC membership have on Irish fisheries?

Documents Resource Book

4. Government, Economy and Society in the Republic of Ireland, 1949–89

Key Concepts and Other Significant Terms

Key Concepts

Balance of Payments
This refers to the difference between the value of exported goods and the value of imported goods in a country. One of the problems facing the Irish economy during the 1950s was caused by the excessive value of imports over exports.

Censorship
Censorship is when the state bans books or films considered to be a danger to (generally) the morals of the people. Although censorship laws were introduced during the 1920s and 1930s, they continued in force until the 1960s.

Common Market
A free trade area in which goods and services can move freely between member states. It was also used as another name for the European Economic Community (EEC) which was founded in 1957 and later developed into the European Union (EU).

Discrimination
Bias against a person or group of people on the basis of factors such as race, gender, sexuality, religion, social class or age. In the Irish context it was often used to describe the treatment of the nationalist minority in Northern Ireland in respect of housing and employment and the treatment of the travelling community in the Republic.

Economic Planning
The establishment by government of economic goals and targets to be achieved over a set period of time. Such economic planning began in Ireland in the late 1950s and was associated particularly with T.K. Whitaker and Seán Lemass.

Ecumenism
This movement among Christians emphasises the common beliefs and traditions rather than the differences between the various Christian churches and works for unity between them.

Equality of Opportunity
This concept means that everyone, regardless of social background, religion or race, will be given the same chance to succeed in life. It particularly refers to the areas of justice, gender, employment and education, and first came to prominence as a political principle during the 1960s.

Free Trade
An economic system in which goods and services can move freely from one country to another, without the imposition of tariffs on imported goods.

Liberalisation
This refers to the establishment of a more open and questioning society that accommodates different points of view, especially in areas such as divorce, contraception and other moral issues. In economic matters it refers to a decrease in state control and the encouragement of private enterprise and competition.

Pluralism
A society that accommodates people of diverse religions, races and points of view.

Secularisation
This refers to a trend in which increasing numbers of people no longer practise religion and the power and influence of the various religious authorities in society grows weaker.

Other Significant Terms

Anglo-Irish Agreement (1985)
This agreement was signed by the British Prime Minister, Margaret Thatcher, and the Taoiseach, Garret FitzGerald in 1985. It provided a consultative role for the Irish Government in Northern Ireland and led to increased co-operation between the British and Irish Governments.

Arms Crisis (1970)
The arms crisis erupted when the Taoiseach, Jack Lynch, sacked two government ministers, Neil Blaney and Charles Haughey, on suspicion of importing arms for use in Northern Ireland. Both men were later found not guilty by the courts. These events resulted in lasting divisions within the Fianna Fáil Party.

Border Campaign of the IRA (1956–62)
This involved attacks, across the border, on RUC barracks in Northern Ireland. It ended in complete failure after both governments – in Northern Ireland and the Republic – introduced internment without trial for members of the IRA.

Broadcasting Ban
Introduced by the Minister for Posts and Telegraphs, Mr Gerry Collins, in 1971, this was a ban on members of the IRA, Sinn Féin or any organisation supporting violence appearing on RTÉ television or radio.

Common Agricultural Policy (EEC)
This guaranteed markets and prices for farm produce throughout the EEC. It was responsible for improvements in the standard of living of Irish farmers.

Common Fisheries Policy (EEC)
Eventually agreed upon by member states in 1983, it set down fishing limits and total allowable catches for all fishermen in the EEC.

Constitutional Crusade (1983)
A largely unsuccessful attempt by the Taoiseach, Garret FitzGerald, to modernise the Irish constitution and to make it more acceptable to Unionists in Northern Ireland.

Declaration of a Republic (1949)
This marked the withdrawal of the state from the British Commonwealth and the establishment of complete sovereignty and independence. Its supporters hoped that it would 'take the gun out of politics' and from then on elections were largely fought on economic rather than on constitutional issues.

Devaluation of Sterling (1949)
As the Irish currency was linked to British sterling, devaluation in Britain also led to a weaker Irish currency, making imported goods much more expensive.

Economic Protection
The form of economic policies pursued in Ireland between 1932 and 1958 involved the protection of Irish industries by the imposition of tariffs on imported goods.

Fiscal Rectitude
This term, which means bringing order to the economy by controlling government spending, was associated particularly with Fine Gael and the Progressive Democrats during the 1980s.

Free Education Scheme (1967)
Introduced by the Fianna Fáil Minister Donogh O'Malley, this involved the provision of free second-level education and means-tested grants for students at third level.

'Gregory Deal' (1982)
This was an agreement between Tony Gregory, a TD for an inner-city constituency in Dublin, and the leader of Fianna Fáil, Charles Haughey. In return for agreeing to vote for Haughey as Taoiseach in the Dáil, Gregory was promised a series of economic improvements for his local area.

International Peace-Keeping Role of the Irish Army
Soon after becoming a member of the United Nations Organisation in 1955, the Irish Army volunteered for peace-keeping duties. Since then members of the Irish Army have given distinguished service in various trouble spots throughout the world.

Inter-Party Government
This term is used when a number of political parties form a government. In Ireland the term has been used exclusively for the governments led by Taoiseach John A. Costello between 1948 and 1951 and between 1954 and 1957.

Ireland Act (1949)
The Ireland Act was a law introduced by the British Government in response to the departure of the Republic from the British Commonwealth. It strengthened partition by guaranteeing that Northern Ireland would remain in the United Kingdom as long as the majority in the Parliament in Belfast so wished.

'Irish Dimension'
Supported by both British and Irish Governments since 1973, this meant that in any settlement in Northern Ireland, the Irish identity of the nationalist minority there had to be respected and taken into account. Under the Anglo-Irish Agreement (1985) this approach was deepened when the Irish Government was given a consultative role in Northern Ireland.

Investment in Education (1965)
This detailed and thorough report by the Organisation of European Co-operation and Development (OECD) on the state of education in Ireland had a profound influence on future developments at all levels of education.

'Just Society' Policy
Although never official party policy, the 'Just Society' proposals of Declan Costello of Fine Gael influenced attitudes to inequality and social divisions in Ireland during the 1960s.

Marriage Ban
This was the rule in many parts of the Irish civil and public services that women had to resign from their jobs when they got married.

Mother and Child Controversy (1951)
A clash between the Minister for Health, Dr Noël Browne, who supported free, universal medical care for mothers and children, and the opponents of the scheme, including the Catholic bishops and most members of the medical profession.

New Ireland Forum
A series of meetings held by constitutional nationalists, from Northern Ireland and the Republic. Its aim was to reach an agreement on a peaceful future for Ireland. It issued its report in May 1984.

Oil Crises (1973 and 1979)
Both the first (1973) and the second oil crisis (1979) began in the Middle East, where oil-producing countries increased the price of oil by huge amounts. This in turn disrupted world economic progress and also seriously damaged the Irish economy.

Power-Sharing
This refers to the idea that any administrations set up in Northern Ireland would have to contain members of both Unionist and Nationalist parties. It was set as a precondition of the restoration of devolved government from the introduction of direct rule in 1972 onwards.

Pro-Life Referendum (1983)
This referendum, which was passed, inserted a clause into the Irish Constitution that conferred a right to life of the unborn, together with an equal right to life of the mother.

Second Vatican Council (1962–65)
The discussions of the council of the Roman Catholic Church held in Rome influenced the way the Catholic Church in Ireland began to come to terms with the modern world.

Sunningdale Agreement (1973)
As a result of this agreement between the British and Irish Governments and political parties in Northern Ireland, a power-sharing executive was established in Northern Ireland. The agreement collapsed following the Ulster workers' strike in May 1974.

Tallaght Strategy (1987)
Alan Dukes, leader of Fine Gael, in a speech in Tallaght in Co. Dublin, agreed to support the minority Fianna Fáil government of Charles Haughey in any measures taken to reduce government spending and set the economy on the path to recovery (see 'fiscal rectitude').

MODERN IRELAND 3RD EDITION

5 Key Personalities

Students are required to study the following key personalities in the section on Government, Economy and Society in the Republic of Ireland, 1949–89:

Archbishop John Charles McQuaid
T.K. Whitaker
Seán Lemass
Gay Byrne
Breandán Ó hEithir
Sylvia Meehan
Jack Lynch
Garret FitzGerald
Charles Haughey
Mary Robinson

Ordinary Level students should focus on the significant landmarks in the person's life, including early influences and career, and the contribution made by him or her to Irish society. Higher Level students should particularly focus on the strengths and weaknesses of the key personalities.

The following is intended to serve as a revision aid to students in studying the key personalities.

Name: Archbishop John Charles McQuaid

Year: 1895–1973

- John Charles McQuaid was President of Blackrock College in Dublin at the time of the Eucharistic Congress in Dublin and advised de Valera on the new Irish Constitution.

- Appointed Catholic Archbishop of Dublin in 1940, he remained in office until 1972. He founded organisations to help the poor and mediated during strikes.

- He was very conservative in outlook. Believing that the Catholic Church should influence society, he was a leading figure in the Mother and Child controversy (1951).

- He was slow to implement changes after the Second Vatican Council and did not support ecumenical connections with other Christian Churches.

32

Name: Seán Lemass

Year: 1899—1971

- A founder member of Fianna Fáil, Lemass was Minister for Industry and Commerce in a number of Fianna Fáil governments during the 1930s and 1950s and advocated a policy of economic self-sufficiency and protectionism.
- During World War II he was appointed Minister for Supplies, with responsibility for rationing and the control and distribution of limited resources.
- On succeeding de Valera as Taoiseach and leader of Fianna Fáil in 1959, Lemass, becoming increasingly convinced of the need for Irish industry to become competitive, adopted the proposals of T.K. Whitaker and set about implementing the First Programme for Economic Expansion.
- The First Programme set targets for growth and set about attracting foreign industries to Ireland by generous tax concessions, leading to dramatic falls in the rates of unemployment and emigration.
- In 1965, he had two historic meetings with the Northern Ireland Prime Minister, Terence O'Neill.
- After presiding over a period of unprecedented economic growth, he resigned as Taoiseach in 1966.

Name: T.K. Whitaker

Year: 1916–

- A public servant and economist, T.K. Whitaker became Secretary of the Department of Finance in 1956.
- He believed that, for Ireland to emerge from the depression of the 1950s, the economy would have to become competitive in an open market, with an emphasis on industrial development.
- He set down his analysis in a paper known as Economic Development, and this became the basis of the First Programme for Economic Expansion, which was implemented by the government of Seán Lemass.
- The First Programme, with its emphasis on an end to protectionism and the promotion of industrial development, helped transform the Irish economy during the 1960s.
- T.K. Whitaker also played a key role in organising the historic meetings between Lemass and the Northern Prime Minister, Terence O'Neill, in 1965.

Name: Gay Byrne

Year: 1934—

- Born in Dublin in 1934 and educated at CBS, Synge Street, Gay Byrne worked in radio and television in Ireland and the UK.
- In 1962 he presented the first *Late Late Show*, which went on to become the longest-running live television chat show in the world.
- The *Late Late Show* helped to change Irish society by providing a forum for open discussion on controversial moral and social issues.
- As well as his television work, he presented the *Gay Byrne* Show on radio, which gave a voice to many people to express their views and air their grievances.
- Gay Byrne received numerous awards as a broadcaster and wrote two books on his experiences: *To Whom it Concerns* and *The Time of My Life*.

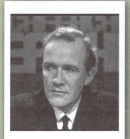

Name: Breandán Ó hEithir

Year: 1930—1991

- Breandán Ó hEithir was a native Irish speaker from the Aran Islands. He went to school and university in Galway.
- He began his career as a newspaper journalist, becoming editor of the Irish language section of the Irish Press in 1957.
- He later became one of the presenters in the Irish language current affairs programme *Féach* on RTÉ television.
- He was very involved in movements to improve the lives of Irish speakers and had a great interest in Gaelic games.
- He published books in both Irish and English on topics such as his own life, sport and politics.

Name: Sylvia Meehan

Year: 1929–

- After graduating from UCD with a degree in legal and political science, Sylvia Meehan qualified as a teacher and was subsequently appointed Vice-Principal of Cabinteely Community School.

- She came to prominence in the 1970s when she left her position as vice-principal to oversee the enforcement of the Employment Equality Act, becoming Chief Executive of the Employment Equality Agency, which was set up in 1977.

- In her role as CEO of the Employment Equality Agency, she highlighted a number of equality issues pertaining to the education of girls and the employment of women.

- She was actively involved in a number of other initiatives and organisations, including the Commission for the Status of Women, Age and Opportunity, the Irish Senior Citizen Parliament, and the European Older People's Platform.

- She received a doctorate from the University of Limerick in 1997.

Name: Jack Lynch

Year: 1917–1999

- Born in Cork in 1917, Jack Lynch became a civil servant in Dublin, where he qualified as a barrister.

- He was elected a Fianna Fáil TD for Cork City in 1948 and was appointed Minister for Education in 1959.

- He was Minister for Finance in 1966 when the Taoiseach Seán Lemass resigned and was elected to lead the Fianna Fáil party.

- As Taoiseach between 1966 and 1973 he dealt with the impact of the Northern Ireland Troubles by calling for a peaceful solution and dismissing ministers during the Arms Crisis in 1970.

- He led Ireland into the EEC in 1973 and returned to power in 1977 with a huge majority.

- Amid growing discontent in the Fianna Fáil party, he resigned as Taoiseach in 1979 and did not approve of his successor as Taoiseach, Charles J. Haughey.

Name: Garret FitzGerald

Year: 1926–2011

- As Minister for Foreign Affairs in the Coalition Government of 1973–77, Garret FitzGerald raised the reputation of Ireland in the EEC.
- He succeeded Liam Cosgrave as leader of Fine Gael in 1977.
- He was Taoiseach in Coalition governments with the Labour Party for two periods: 1981–82 and 1982–87.
- He was an advocate of social change, such as divorce, but his governments failed to solve the economic problems of the 1980s.
- His main success was the signing of the Anglo-Irish Agreement (1985), which prepared the way for future peace in Northern Ireland.

Name: Charles Haughey

Year: 1925–2006

- A member of Fianna Fáil since 1948, Charles Haughey served as Minister for Justice, Minister for Agriculture and Minister for Finance in a number of governments during the 1960s.

- In 1970 he was dismissed from the cabinet by the Taoiseach, Jack Lynch, for failing to support government policy on Northern Ireland. Subsequently, he was acquitted of all charges to conspire to import arms illegally to aid Northern nationalists.

- Having spent some time in the political wilderness, he was appointed opposition spokesman for health in 1975 and became Minister for Health and Social Welfare following the 1977 general election.

- He defeated his arch-rival George Colley to succeed Jack Lynch as Taoiseach and leader of Fianna Fáil in 1979.

- His government failed to come to grips with the worsening state of the public finances and his personal style of leadership remained very controversial and divisive. From 1982 to 1987 Haughey was leader of the opposition.

- Haughey broke Fianna Fáil tradition by entering a coalition government with the Progressive Democrats in 1989 and began to deal successfully with the country's economic problems.

- He resigned in 1992 following controversy over the earlier tapping of journalists' telephones.

Name: Mary Robinson

Year: 1944–

- During a long and distinguished career, Mary Robinson was a barrister, a politician, and President of Ireland.
- She had an esteemed reputation as a constitutional lawyer and was involved in many high-profile cases in the European courts in relation to issues such as access to legal aid and the decriminalisation of homosexual activities.
- Elected to the Seanad in 1969, she later joined the Labour Party but failed to win a seat to the Dáil on a number of occasions.
- She left the Labour Party following the signing of the Anglo-Irish Agreement, but was nominated by the Labour Party as a presidential candidate and was elected Ireland's first woman President in 1990.
- She transformed the role of the President, taking a special interest in Irish emigrants, poverty and human rights issues.
- She resigned as President in November 1997 to take up a new position as UN High Commissioner for Human Rights.

For permission to reproduce photographs, the authors and publisher gratefully acknowledge the following: © Alamy: 33, 39; © Getty: 34, 37, 40; Courtesy of the Irish Defence Forces: 22; © Irish Examiner: 11; © National Gallery of Ireland / NGI.4204: 229, Simon Elwes, British, 1902–1975 / The Most Reverend John Charles McQuaid, Archbishop of Dublin and Primate of Ireland, 1969 / Oil on canvas / 127 x 102 cm / © Artist's Estate Courtesy of the National Library of Ireland: 12, 17, 19, 20; © RTÉ Stills Library: 17, 35T, 35B, 36, 38.

The authors and publisher have made every effort to trace all copyright holders, but if any has been inadvertently overlooked we would be pleased to make the necessary arrangement at the first opportunity.